THE JOURNEY OF A DOLLAR

ILLUSTRATED BY
HOWARD FRIDSON

WRITTEN BY
DORIS RUBENSTEIN

BEAVER'S POND
PRESS

AFFINITY PLUS
FEDERAL CREDIT UNION

Thanks to Affinity Plus Federal Credit Union for its belief in this story and its generosity for publication.

ISBN: 978-1-59298-793-1
Library of Congress Catalog Number: 2016912093
Printed in the United States of America
First Printing: 2016
20 19 18 17 16   5 4 3 2 1

Illustration by Howard Fridson
Edited by Lily Coyle
Book design and typesetting by Dan Pitts

BEAVER'S POND
PRESS

Beaver's Pond Press
7108 Ohms Lane
Edina, MN 55439–2129
(952) 829-8818
www.BeaversPondPress.com

Dedications

To Siona, who asked the question.
—D.R.

To old friends, the best kind.
—H.F.

4

Chapter 1

"What can I do for a dollar?" Elliot asked his mother at breakfast one Saturday.

"You can download an app to play a game," his mother replied.

"No, that's not what I mean!" Elliot said. "I mean, what can I do to earn a dollar?"

5

"Why do you need to earn a dollar?" his mother asked.

Elliot explained that his class was studying Ecuador. They wanted to help the poor children there. The teacher asked everyone to work to earn a dollar to send to Ecuador.

Elliot's mother thought for a minute. What did she need to have done around the house that Elliot could do to earn a dollar? What kind of work was worth a dollar? How long should it take to do that work that would be worth a dollar?

The sun was shining brightly that day. She would ask him to do something outside of the house. She thought of something that Elliot could do and be finished within thirty minutes.

"Elliot, there are weeds in my flowerbeds," she said. "If you will pull the weeds for a half-hour, I will pay you a dollar."

Elliot liked helping his mother plant flowers every spring. They planted zinnias and cosmos with seeds. They took little seedlings of marigolds and impatiens from small pots and replanted them in the ground. Elliot was always proud when the flowers grew and made their house look pretty.

"That's a great idea!" he shouted and he ran to get his garden tools.

What's your favorite flower?

7

8

Chapter 2

Elliot put on his gloves to keep his hands from getting too dirty. He used a cultivator to make the soil loose so that he could pull the weeds easily. It was not easy to pull some of the weeds and others had prickly needles on them. He pulled a pile of weeds and threw them on the compost heap in a corner of the yard.

When he finished, he showed his mother what he had done. She was very happy with his work and gave him a crisp, new dollar bill.

"You made the garden more beautiful than ever!" she told Elliot. He was very proud of doing a good job. And then she gave him two quarters. "This is a tip for you for being such a good son and gardener. You did much more than I expected you to do."

That night and the next night, Elliot slept with his dollar under his pillow and his two quarters in a jar on his dresser.

On Monday morning, Elliot took the bus to school. He touched the pocket in his shirt every few minutes to make sure that the dollar was still there.

He looked around and wondered how many of his classmates on the bus had earned money over the weekend and had a dollar in their pocket.

What could YOU do to earn a dollar to give to help someone in need?

Chapter 3

That afternoon, Elliot's mother came to school, too. It was her turn to be a teacher's assistant. She came to Elliot's class.

When the time came for the lesson on Ecuador, the teacher, Mr. Curran, asked each child to come to the front of the room with their dollar to tell what they had done to earn it.

LaToya earned her dollar by walking her little sister in the stroller when her parents were painting the porch.

Sophia earned her dollar by washing out the family's garbage cans and recycling bins.

Each time a student told their story of earning money, they put the dollar in a big jar on Mr. Curran's desk.

When it was Elliot's turn, he told how he had pulled weeds in the hot sun.

"There are many poor children in Ecuador who work all day pulling weeds in the potato fields and cannot go to school," Mr. Curran told the class.

Mr. Curran had lived in Ecuador many years before as a Peace Corps volunteer.

Elliot said, "I'm glad that I can help those children go to school with my dollar." And he proudly put it into the jar. His mother smiled. She was very proud of Elliot, too.

That night, when his mother came to tuck him in, Elliot said, "I put my dollar in the jar at school today. But how is my dollar going to get to Ecuador to help the little children who can't go to school because they have to pull weeds in the potato fields?"

Elliot's mother smiled and looked at him with love. "Close your eyes," she said, "and I'll tell you about the journey that dollar is taking to Ecuador."

Did you take a trip somewhere last summer?

15

16

Chapter 4

First, Elliot's mother asked him to name all the students in his class.

"There's Sophia, LaToya, Abdi, and the twins, Ari and Ariana, Brooke, Hannah, Mack, Sadie, and …" Elliot went on until he had named all 23 children in his class. "And me!"

"So there are 24 dollars in the jar," said Elliot's mother.

"No!" cried Elliot, opening his eyes. "Mr. Curran gave a dollar, too! There are 25 dollars!"

"The first thing that will happen is that Mr. Curran will take the 25 dollars and put a rubber band around them. He will take the dollars to the school office so that he can write a letter," Elliot's mother said. And she was right.

Here's what Mr. Curran's letter said:

"Dear Friends,

These 25 dollars are from my second grade class at MacDowell Elementary School. We are studying Ecuador. We would like to help children in Ecuador to have a better life."

Elliot's mother continued, "He will sign the letter and write down the name of each child who gave a dollar. Then he will put the letter and money in a big envelope and send it to New York City."

"But I want my dollar to go to Ecuador – not New York City!" said Elliot and opened his eyes wide.

"Be calm!" his mother requested. "In New York City, the dollars from your class will be delivered to a special charity group that helps children in Ecuador and other countries around the world. There, it will meet 25 dollars from children in a school in California.

It will meet 15 dollars from children in a church Sunday School class from Tennessee.

It will meet 35 dollars that was sent by children in Michigan who put on a play for their neighbors over the summer to earn money."

How much money is that, including the 25 dollars from Elliot's class?

Chapter 5

"So, my dollar has gone from our house to my school and then to New York City!" Elliot said with excitement.

He had never been to New York City but he had seen pictures of it in books and on television. With his eyes closed, he could see the tall buildings and the Statue of Liberty. He could see the door of an office in one of the buildings. He imagined his dollar sitting on a big desk in the charity's office in one of those tall buildings.

"But how does my dollar go from New York to Ecuador?" he asked. Elliot was anxious for his dollar to arrive in Ecuador safely.

His mother said that the dollar now went from the charity's office into a big bank downtown. Elliot had been downtown with his mother to a big bank building. It had a very high ceiling and marble pillars at the doorway.

"In the bank," Elliot's mother continued, "your dollar and the other 99 dollars get put into a special place with money that hundreds and hundreds of other people have given to the charity to help people in need."

Elliot's eyes popped open. "I bet there's a jillion dollars from the charity in that bank!"

His mother laughed. "Not quite. But there are many millions. Still, your dollar is very special."

Elliot smiled as he closed his eyes again.

"The next day," Elliot's mother explained, "a person who works for the charity group in Ecuador will be able to use that money to help children who need it."

She asked Elliot if he remembered seeing her or his father write checks to pay bills. Sometimes, too, they used the Internet to pay bills with a credit card number.

"Of course," he said. Elliot knew that his parents put money in the bank or their credit union and then used checks and debit cards instead of dollar bills to pay for things.

His mother kissed him good night.

As he drifted off to sleep, he pictured a woman who looked like his mother (only with red hair because Elliot liked red hair) carrying his dollar from the charity's office to a bank very much like the one downtown.

Does your family have an account at a bank or a credit union?

23

NEW YORK

QUITO

BANK

BANCO

24

Chapter 6

That morning at breakfast, Elliot had one more question. "I don't understand something," Elliot told his mother. "How does the charity lady in Ecuador get the money from the bank in New York?"

"Good question!" said his mother. "The bank in New York City has a branch – sort of a sister bank – in Quito, the capital city of Ecuador. When the charity puts money in their New York City account, another person who works for the charity in Ecuador can go to the *sister bank* called a *branch* in Ecuador. She can take out the money there to use it for the school children."

"A branch," Elliot whispered, and closed his eyes while he chewed his toast. He pictured a big tree with a tall, wide trunk and many branches. There was no money on the trunk, but instead of leaves on the tree, there were dollar bills.

"Oh!" he gasped. "Do they use dollars in Ecuador? I know that they don't use them in England." Elliot's cousin studied in England and gave him some English money when she returned. "Why, yes, they do use dollars in Ecuador!" his mom said. "Only a few countries outside of the United States use American dollars, and Ecuador is one of them."

Elliot breathed easy now.

His dollar was safely on its way to Ecuador and it didn't have to travel on a jet or in a car where it might get lost or stolen.

Can you find England on a map or globe?
What is the capital of England?

THE EQUATOR

☆ QUITO

Ecuador

THE TROPICAL RAINFOREST

THE ANDES MOUNTAINS

THE PACIFIC OCEAN

28

Chapter 7

Elliot and his class continued to learn about Ecuador. They knew that it was in South America. They learned that Ecuador has a long coast along the Pacific Ocean. They learned that the Andes mountains run down the center of the country. And they learned about the wild tropical rain forest in the eastern part of the country.

Elliot wrote a report on the toucan. It's a bird with a large, colorful beak that lives in Ecuador. But he kept wondering where his dollar ended up.

One day, just before school ended for the summer, Mr. Curran brought a letter to read to the class. It had a beautiful stamp on the envelope.

The letter was from a woman in Ecuador who worked for the charity that received Elliot's dollar.

Mr. Curran read the letter. It said that the money from Elliot's class went to the village of La Esperanza in the Andes mountains of Ecuador.

Mr. Curran took out the map of Ecuador that the class had used all year. He asked Jessica to come to the front to point to La Esperanza on the map.

Can you find Ecuador on a map or globe?

Chapter 8

The letter said that their dollars were used to provide school supplies to a school in La Esperanza for grades one through three. The lady sent a picture of the school and the schoolchildren. On the back of the picture were the names of all of the children.

"Thanks to each and every child in Mr. Curran's class who contributed a dollar to help the pupils," the lady wrote. "There used to be no school near here, so children worked all day in the potato fields. Now there is a school and a teacher, but most parents are so poor that they cannot pay for supplies like pencils or notebooks or crayons."

Elliot thought back about his dollar. What a journey it had made! It went from his house

to his school

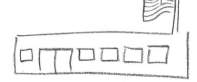

to New York City where it went to the office of the charity organization

to a big bank in New York

to a bank in Quito, and then

to a school in La Esperanza.

Elliot sat back in his desk and closed his eyes.

He could see a little boy sitting in a school desk in La Esperanza. The boy looked a lot like him. And both of them were smiling.

Will you join Elliot in helping people in need to have a better, happier life? How?

Resources

Here are some ideas of things YOU can do to raise money to help people in need:
- Have a refreshment stand in front of your house or at a sporting event in your neighborhood.
- Organize your friends to put on a talent show and sell tickets.
- Be like Elliot and his classmates and do lawn and garden chores for your family or neighbors.
- Have a car wash in your driveway.

Always make sure to have a sign that tells why you are doing your project and which organization will send the money on the journey to help others.

Here are some trusted national charities:
- American Red Cross
- St. Jude Hospital for Children
- Make-a-Wish Foundation
- United Way

These are trusted international charities:
- CARE
- U.S. Committee for UNICEF
- American Refugee Committee

Want to learn about "Super-Giver" philanthropists?
Go to this website:
http://www.biography.com/people/groups/philanthropists

What are some important charity organizations in YOUR community?

36

HOWARD FRIDSON is an illustrator living in Huntington Woods, Michigan, around the block from the rhinoceroses at the Detroit Zoo. He and his wife, Cathy, met in the ninth grade and began dating only thirteen years later. They have three grown sons, Nate, Blake, and Russell. Howard graduated from Wayne State University in 1971 with a degree in fine arts and has been creating artwork ever since. His pieces range in size from dollhouse miniatures to three-story murals. In 1992 Howard and his friend Martin Scot Kosins produced *Maya's First Rose*, which hit number one on the *Detroit Free Press* bestseller list. Howard and Doris first collaborated on a 1969 theatre production as camp counselors. This is their second opportunity to work together.

DORIS RUBENSTEIN spent her entire career in the field of philanthropy and is the author of a book for grown-ups called *The Good Corporate Citizen: A Practical Guide*. Her fans call her "The Giving Guru." Doris really knows how your charity dollar travels, having served as a Peace Corps volunteer in Ecuador and later working as a fundraiser for CARE, one of the world's oldest international aid and development organizations. Her expertise and knowledge of fundraising and the non-profit world won her two awards from the University of Minnesota Alumni Association and a prestigious Kenneth E. Clark Award from the Center for Creative Leadership. Doris received her B.A. from the University of Michigan and an M.A. from Augsburg College. A native of Detroit, Michigan, she's called Minnesota home since 1984. Doris and Howard met as summer camp counselors in 1969. They're thrilled to work together to bring this important story to children.

37